A Space Between Rains

A Space
Between Rains

Love Poems about
endings
and beginnings

Victoria Chames

Other Books by this author:
Inchworms: Poems, Sketches and Stories

NuSPACE-082225

978-0-9714359-2-6

Darkhorse Press U.S.
Oakland California 94609
www.darkhorsepress.com

For Amanda Belle Long
my birth mother Ann,
who would have loved
to sing and dance,
but never did.

Table of Contents

Part Three

Part One

I Have Chosen You

I am with you
because I have chosen to be,
and not because of anything
you have done
or ever will do.
I have chosen you,
it is my choice to make,
and I make it every day.
I am with you from day to day
because I have traveled enough to know
that only the heart is home
and even that
only for moments at a time.
Because I am wise enough to know
that a giving man
is a thing of great value,
I give to you, again and again
my unassailable, unstealable self,
each day new,
because I have chosen you.

A Pure and Perfect Love

You're so beautiful
when you're glad -
warm and loving,
sharing everything you've got
with me.
But when your mood is dark,
you draw back
and close yourself,
angry and hurt
and sullen as a child.
You are unreachable,
unbearable,
and totally, utterly
impossible.
And me, well I'm always
complicated;
I never was easy
to love.
But Nobody else
could love any better.
Nobody has
a pure and perfect love.
We're all fragmented
and full of flaws.

It's the Law
of Scenario Universe.
But all of the pieces,
if brought together
with all of the flaws,
would fit together
perfectly.
It's mostly a matter
of finding all the parts.
I love you in joy
and I love you in anger,
and even when I cannot touch you,
I can feel you still.
And we may never get it right
but we will find some perfect parts,
and we probably are about as pure
as it gets.

The Honing Edge

Look at October's brilliant skies—
they ache with beauty,
and fluttering flocks of yellow leaves
sailing down the wind
like migrating birds.
The heart must wonder
what the winter will hold,
for winter is the honing edge
that sharpens the soul.
I see you changing,
though I've tried not to see.
I always thought we would
change together,
grow together,
like the ivy and the cypress.
But nothing in life is guaranteed,
and nothing is more constant
among living things
than growing and changing.
And so we find out,
that life is not so easy
as it always seemed
on those long golden evenings
of timeless summer.

Come November,
the gold becomes silver,
and the air is thin.
The dark comes down so suddenly,
and if you're caught out,
the chill after sunset
can cut you to the bone.

Things Ending

There's something comfortable
in common things
that are routine, a reassurance.
The blurred sound of engines
outside in the dark,
pleasantly anonymous
in their familiarness,
or a droning voice
that was always in the background.
There is a sudden hurt
in the taking away
of something that seemed unchangeable;
a sharp drawing-in of breath
at the unexpected silence
of things ending,
things made noticeable by their absence
that were nearly invisible
in their presence.
The resonant ringing ghost
of something newly gone
is like a hole in the air,
like a space in the wind,
like waking in the night to the sound of
a sound ceasing.

Forever -1

Forever is not a pendulum
that once set in motion
swings contentedly.
Forever is a momentary act
that must be created
and re-created
each moment
for eternity.

The Likes of That

Her lashes were so very
sudden and dark,
a man is lost against
the likes of that.
I would understand
and forgive it,
he's saying to himself.

"A man is only a man.
She's said it herself,
many times.
She knows I care."

That's what I hear him saying
in his mind
as he follows her
up the stairs.

Unforgiven

I am so hurt, I will not show it.
In fact, I will throw it
in their faces, for spite.
I'll wear my red dress,
and dark-painted eyes,
and completely disguise
the hole in my life.
But after the party
when I come back here,
I'll strip off my armor
and melt down the mask
I've learned to wear,
and lie down alone
to cry bitter tears into my hair.

When Love Is Ending

When love is ending, it will end.
We do the love an injustice
to hold it together
with excuses
and old habits.
Love never was
meant to be unchanging.
Love never does
fit the old clothes.
Sometimes a long love
is close enough to forever;
sometimes it comes and goes
as willfully as the winds.
The fact that love ends
in no way diminishes
what it was, while it was.
When love ends
it should end gently,
so what lingers lies lightly,
not heavily,
on the heart.

After Goodbye

Loneliness comes down
with the twilight
and settles quietly
into the room,
while silence in fine particles
drops like dust
sifting through air,
settling too,
till every unmoving thing
is covered with it.
I wait for dark,
and sleep is
my only escape from
the absence of you.

Something In You

What has been
has cost me pain
critical enough to make me know
how foolish I was,
would be, to go
that way again.
There is no reason for me to say
I love you
any longer.
You are unreachable;
for me to wonder
whether you remember
to wear your scarf
and turn up your collar
against the wind
is a useless thing
to clutter my mind
when you are so clearly
behind me now.
It's just that there was
something in you
that something in me still
reaches out to,
no matter what I do.

Night Rain

It's better to spend a lifetime alone
than spend a lifetime lying.
God what a melancholy wind
is heaving the trees around–
this sudden deluge of unrelenting rain,
still coming down.

The sky is gray and heavy as slate.
Blasted by winds, the naked branches
twist in their torment like a snared beast
caught a net.

Well it is warm enough here where I am,
though I can't say that it always was;
and anyway, each of us has
our own torment.

The River in Winter

Until I came back here
to this frozen river shore
buried in blown snow
and locked into silence,
I had forgotten
how bitter winter was.
How the ravaging of winds in a rage
tore at my face
like teeth and claws,
stabbing my eyes
till they poured with tears
swept back at once into my hair,
for the winds will not let them
flow casually down
a pink-flushed cheek
like ordinary, indoor cheers,
or summer tears,
or the gentle tears of
someone touched by love.

Cross-Country

I want to ski
a hard hundred miles,
wrapped in light
and weighing nothing,
with nothing before me but
smooth white silence
and nothing behind me but
strange songs on the wind
like the songs of the sea.
And you,
somewhere warm in the arms
of another lover
can never
touch me.

Part Two

Free

And so it gets lonely
in the middle of sleep,
waking from a warm dream
that was a dream only.
I make my way,
my life is my own,
but still I remember
how good it was to feel
a warm live man
in my bed,
especially in winter
when the darkness aches.
But I'm okay, I'm a survivor,
that's what they tell me.
I'm not in trouble,
not out of luck.
I'm just a little too free.
But isn't that the hell of it—
everybody's so busy
being so free,
they hardly have time to notice
how empty it is.

Directions

An oddly quiet, stillborn day.
The morning is sunless;
a colorless haze
veils the low hills.
Beneath the flat sky,
the grass is pale,
as if summer's ghost
had passed through here,
stilling the air
and silencing birds,
while everything that lives
seems waiting.
I have come to the middle of my life,
as well as we are given to know,
and I asked directions
at the side of the road.
I was told "Go on;
There is no other way
to go."

Winter Sun

I spent a long time learning,
and what have I learned?
Mostly that there are things
that cannot be known.
I spent a lifetime seeking,
and what have I gained?
Only the space of time,
and the miles I came.
Last night the sun came out
from underneath the rain,
breaking through,
only to sink again.
Last night the sun came out
just before it set.
Sometimes it feels like
my life has been
like that

Just Like a Lover

Blond and tall, just like a lover
is supposed to look,
with a quiet manner
and a strong proud face.
You took me with such dignity
and unexpected grace,
and when you slept,
your mouth
turned up at the corners
in the most mysterious smile
like those ancient Greek statues.
I watched you sleeping and
thought to leave,
to slip away in darkness
and seal you in silence
with the love behind your eyes
and your strange ancient smile.
But when I rose to go,
my weariness overwhelmed me.
The room spun around slowly
and the cold air rushed at me;
I crept back gratefully to
your pool of warmth.
In the morning we parted
with few words,

discreet kisses,
and what I took for
meaningful glances.
I walked up the hallway
with strong bold strides,
but as cool and nonchalant
as I tried to be,
a tear or two trickled down.
But I didn't turn to look back,
so you didn't see.

The Way The Wind

Look at the way the wind
tears at the trees,
and the mottled sky
floats in its disorder,
stirred together
with yesterday's clouds,
perfect clouds
shattered and broken now,
strewn across a bleak expanse
behind the torn trees.
Look at the way the wind
scatters brown leaves,
scraping like fingernails
on concrete walks,
their brittle sounds, louder now,
at this pale hour of morning
when no one is abroad.
All summer long,
the wind meandered,
wandering careless,
warm and kind.
There is solemn warning in
the way the wind
changes its mind.

Today Loving

Let today's troubles
be sufficient for today.
My mind aches weary
and my body aches restless.
When I am locked, delirious
in our passionate struggle,
throwing my soul
and my body against yours,
I never think then
in terms of time and space.
I never think at all.
Something primitive
is let loose in me
and blossoms like a bursting flame.
When it subsides,
I am grateful, and peaceful,
and returned to myself again,
spent and exhausted,
and sane.

No Strings

We were terrific—
What great breakers
and waves of rapture
washed over me
when we made love;
it was the best of
whatever it was.
But that was mostly
all we had.
There never was much of
touching with the eyes,
or hearts, or minds.
Ours was a sensible
adult arrangement:
plenty of freedom
and all the good things,
with no strings attached,
being careful not to care.
And when I looked for
something deeper,
it just wasn't there.

Just Before Sleep

Just before sleep
I am a time-traveler.
I still remember
all the old places
the mind returns to
but the heart dares not enter.
I still remember
all the closed faces:
people who saw me every day
and thought they knew me.
I passed through the periphery
of their lives
like any common stranger
taking a short-cut across the lawn
who, reaching the sidewalk again,
goes on.

Untitled

It was the tenderest
gentle kiss—
not the usual peck on the cheek
from my old friend.
I almost felt something
stirring in me,
like a sweet small shock,
the kind I got
at seventeen.
Such a little kiss,
yet It lingered on my mouth
hours after
he had left,
and when I fell asleep
I thought of it,
and when I woke in the morning
I remembered it.

I Come To You

I come to you
to look into your eyes,
knowing that you may never give me
anything more.
But the love that goes out from me
comes back from you
gentle and warm,
strong and steady as your gaze,
like the love that little children give,
so honest and open,
so unaware.
I come to you
to look into your eyes
because there is so much
kindness there,
it's like standing near
the fire.

Just Friends

What can I write for you
as a friend,
that you might understand
the sweet lingering ache
your affection gives me,
your innocent small kisses
that flicker like candles
in my unlighted soul.
Even a little fire
is dangerous
in such a dry year.

Moment

You were as graceful as a deer,
standing naked in the morning
groping for your clothes,
nothing but muscle and bone,
and lean as a sprinter.
In a moment or less
you were dressed and gone
out the door,
and I watched after you
from deep in the covers.
Gone like only a glint of light
that one small square inch
of universe catches
just for an instant,
so beautiful and so brief,
the eye hardly knows for sure
it was there at all.

The One That Got Away

Something really broke last night,
and I fell through.
I went to bed, so depressed,
after having had words with you.
I have not fallen quite so deep
into the spiral of my own soul,
of my own silence, for a lifetime.
It was as if a veil were drawn back
and vision became so utterly clear,
it was all I could bear.
I saw naked, life's contradictions,
pleasure and pain,
and the nature of love.
But then, as quickly as it had come,
it slipped away.
In poetry we often speak of
things like loneliness, love, and sorrow,
but nothing is glimpsed
for more than an instant,
a flickering moment
that blinks like a firefly,
and then sails away into the night,
faster than the fastest pen
can write.

Charlie

Charlie's gone.
The winter settles in.
Dry leaves curl
and drop and skitter
in concrete gutters
and crunch like cornflakes,
cornflake brown.
It doesn't seem to matter much
now that he's gone.
Charlie was a charming little cat,
black and white, just half grown.
He never even got the chance
to become worldly,
a macho Tom.
Cats aren't very smart about cars.
To cross the street,
they crouch way down and run,
straight as an arrow,
looking neither right nor left
and trying to be
invisible.
Sadly, sometimes
It doesn't work.
I too, seem to do things

the same old
not-so-good way,
make the same mistakes
with lovers and friends
again and again.
Charlie and I were innocent
of anything but
good intentions.
But the summer came and went,
and I am still alone,
and Charlie's gone.

Winterlong

There is a kind of love
that wanders blind
like blown leaves,
a love that longs to lie down
in mud or snow or rain
and be allowed some dignity
in which to die.
Dry leaves catch in gutter grates
and scrape along the sidewalk cracks
and finally find a stopping place
to wait for spring.
But this love falls
and never finds a ground,
endlessly flies in empty wind
the winter long, long into spring
and cannot cling
to any living thing.

Winter Walking

I remember Minnesota,
ink-blue light of midnight sky
reflected on snow,
the tight squeak and crunch
of exquisite powder
beneath my boot-steps,
the sharp sting and ache
of vicious winds
numbing my face.
The rest of me
completely enclosed
against bitter cold.
Safe-sheltered
in wool and down,
in mittens and parka,
in jeans and long-johns,
snow-boots,
and thick wool socks.
A knitted wool hat,
a knit scarf on top of that,
wrapped around my neck
to my nose.
I remember those
long winter nights,

and my winter walks
that were almost like prayer.
On the bridge, by the river,
and the railroad trestle.
Walk fast; it helps
defend against the cold,
and if it is very cold,
run.
But if it is only
a little cold,
like ten-below,
go silent, go holy,
go thoughtfully slow
through the whispering drifts,
immaculate
and soft as ghosts
or angels, shifting
in mysterious winds,
my sacred companions,
all along the long walk
home.

Dream

It was only a dream that woke me
in the stillness of the night,
only a memory unwinding in sleep
that brought back the silence and the light,
and the image of a face I knew
as well as I know my own
came back for a moment and kissed my eyes
and woke me, and was gone.

Morning Rain

Rain in the morning half-light,
a holding of breath, without mood.
Soft, strange, and innocent as
the look caught from
a stranger in passing,
someone you will not see again,
and never touch.

Because of what has gone before
and what I have learned from that,
I need less time to make a mistake
and have grown agile
in turning around
to go another way.

The Gypsy

When Mama was young,
she used to sing gypsy songs
from the radio,
about gypsy-girl dancers
and wild gypsy lovers
with dark smoldering eyes
and beautiful names.
But she married a man
and my brother and I were born
and she spent the best of her life trying
to play the role of mother,
not dancer.
I too chose to marry,
and played the part too well,
and too long,
until the greenest years of my life
were gone.
When I broke away,
it was not without pain,
but I just couldn't stand
the loneliness any longer.
And so I have wandered
all these years
and known many lovers,
each lonelier than the last,

and even the best of them
had little to give me.
I am the gypsy
Mama always wanted to be
and never was.

Petit Amour

I remember it – nearly summer,
one magnificent, sunshiny day
we came out to the emerald fields and farms
with other friends, to play.
The river ran and the songbirds sang,
and everything was bliss.
We considered each other, and wanted to,
but we had not yet kissed.

We lay on our backs on the top of a hill
underneath the sky,
touching each other so eagerly,
but only with our eyes;
my eyes green as the riverbank,
and yours the color
of a storm at sea.
I loved you then as I love you still,
mon cheval joli.

Forever 2

But you know how it is with
forever,
you can never
nail it down,
not even if you
get it in writing.
Forever always finds the means
to slip the noose and get away,
leaving you with
all you ever really had,
that is, today,
to try to make a life with,
which is, after all,
at least a little piece
of forever.

Solitude

My solitude is a patient friend,
neither giving nor asking an answer.
The curtains drift on a tentative wind,
and the room where I lay with my lover
is empty now. Whatever it was,
it's over.

Part Three

Promises

A kite pulls against the string
struggling upwards,
soaring.
Although the length
and the strength of the string
measure the limits
of its flight,
it is exactly that
tension against the wind
that powers it.
Pushing and pulling,
both at once,
like love and commitment,
earth and sky are tied together.
This tension must be;
for when the string breaks,
the soaring stops
abruptly.
The kite hesitates
and hangs in mid-air,
shuddering a moment,
then spiraling down.
Without that connection,
to climb the brave skies

is impossible.
Just as, without promises,
love can only flutter a little,
incapable of flight.
Love is like
a law of physics.
It just works like that.

Woman / Haiku

49

I am strong
like the green bamboo,
the unassuming graceful stem
that bows to many things.
Cold steel shatters, finally,
but the bamboo bends
in the fiercest winds
and rises again,
and again.

The Commonest Word

Divorce is perhaps the commonest word
in cocktail conversation.
I've left that behind me.
I no longer wear my little black dress,
elegant but simple.
I don't care for parties
with drinks and small-talk,
I am older and no longer
pay those dues.

The divorce was almost an afterthought,
the leaving was the hard part,
tearing away from the safety and silence
of a long non-life.
That was the price
of a raffle-ticket chance
to seek and to find
a life again.

When I tore my soul free,
what was left of me,
A profusion of pain
and unimagined blood
burst out; I thought

I would not heal.
But time would finally
seal the wound,
and loneliness provide new pain
to cauterize the old pain clean.

Now no more blood
or other oozing stuff
is there anymore,
and even the scars have faded.
Where there was pain,
there is peacefulness.
Where there was hurt,
forgiveness,
for both of us.
Ten years are gone
since the day my spirit broke,
and I surprise myself to find
I am clean
and whole.

Freedom

Freedom doesn't live in a bachelor flat
or a rented room painted white,
stacked with books and objets d'art
the way we all lived in New York.
To be without attachments
has nothing to do with
being free,
and I can speak with some authority
on the subject of freedom,
in all its faces, all its disguises.
It's not the same
as loneliness.
Though loneliness is often
the asking-price,
it's not impossible
for bargains to be made.

To go it alone in many bright cities,
"the strange dark woman
from out of town"
was exciting and brave;
it fed my blood.
But something was always eluding me,
dancing away

like ripples on a rain-pool.
The secrets of scenario universe
slipping away like water,
through the smallest imaginable
chink in my armor.

Freedom doesn't live
anyplace you can go;
freedom is a soul-thing
that only the heart knows.
If it's not there,
you're not going to find it
anywhere.

The Love I Meant

Late last night
I remembered again
things I forgot a lifetime ago.
The love we had or didn't have.
What it was, or what it wasn't,
I still don't know.
It ended at the beginning
and you never noticed.
The love I meant, you never knew,
because you never wanted to.
The love I meant,
well, it was like
turning off the light,
and the presence still there
in soft brown shadows,
as if I were not invisible,
as if I were not always alone.
As if you were not
always, always,
gone.

To Love a Stranger

It's easier
to love a stranger,
someone I can be sure
doesn't care,
someone who cannot possibly know
the times and the ways
I've failed before.
Someone who can hurt me
only so much,
and whether he loves me or not,
doesn't matter.
Someone accepting any old lie
I care to offer,
and if I don't bother,
accepting that too.
It was easier to love
all of my strangers
than it ever was to love you.

Looking Back

As I turn the last time to look back again,
I count the times on less than a hand
when even for a moment there had been
a bond between us.
I forgive you as I let you go,
you thought you gave nothing,
you didn't know
that needing is a kind of giving too.
Maybe I loved you better than you knew.
Go on then, go the way you will,
beautiful boy, you never could be still.
You never loved me, now you never will.

A Space Between Rains

Sometimes in spring
when the heavy rains come,
there's a break in the weather
for a moment,
or an hour,
when the storm relents.
A quiet space
when everything seems to hesitate
in unbelief, and
breathing the most imperceptible sigh,
gathers itself together
to be ready
for the next downpour.
It is this gentle
space between rains
that I ask of you now
for my own gathering.

Other Rains

I remember other rains
more beautiful,
more delicate than this.
I've known so many
soft gray afternoons
waiting out the rain
in some dim room
alone, or in the warmth of a lover,
while the wallpaper flowers
stared down at us
in their odd old-fashioned way
and the hours seemed timeless
as the winds rose and fell
and the rains subsided,
swept and spattering,
tap-dancing on the roof,
as afternoon drifted
into twilight.
Soft rains have taught me
the beauty of subtlety
and quiet things.
Not everything is a poem;
some things simply are
what they are.

The River In Spring

I come so quietly
even the birds
hardly notice me,
nor hurry to leave
their business in the brambles.
My old friend the river
is greatly changed
by the rains this year.
Trees torn down
are thrown across the banks
like misplaced beams
intended for building
something
that was later reconsidered
and abandoned.
What new wonders
the waters have wrought–
hillsides have slid into lower plateaus,
and the river moves over
without complaint
to different levels and boundaries
as we all must
when time changes things.

Forever - 3

Love is more wonderful
than just about anything,
but when we're enraptured
in the magic of it,
we tend to forget
that forever never happens
except
one minute at a time,
starting now.

Nearly Summer

Every year the summer
comes like love,
as if it had never come before
and never would again.
After the months of rain, the sun
beginning in the solar plexus
warms me from
within.

The Beginning

About the Author

Victoria Chames is an artist, poet, and writer
living in Northern California and currently working
on the memoir trilogy
Victory Is My Name

To contact the author, email to:
spacebetween@darkhorsepress.com

About Darkhorse Press

We are a Small Press in the time-honored tradition of
American authors and self-publishers like Henry David
Thoreau, Ralph Waldo Emerson, Walt Whitman, and others.
Small Presses and self-publishing have always been a
respected part of American Literature.

Darkhorse Press U.S.
http://www.darkhorsepress.com